Introduction

The North Yorkshire Moors Railway has been the north-east's premier heritage railway for decades and is, in fact, Britain's most visited steam line, carrying over 300,000 passengers every year.

Some steam railways offer a couple of miles trundling past uninspiring landscapes at a pedestrian rate. The NYMR, however, can boast 18 miles of track passing through spectacular scenery in a national park, with many trains running the extra 6 miles alongside the pretty River Esk to the coast at Whitby, sharing this route with Northern Rail services from Middlesbrough. As such, the NYMR is the only heritage line to run a regular service on the National Rail network.

There are walks to waterfalls and Roman remains, and there are friendly pubs and tearooms to discover along the way. From the castle at Pickering through the glaciated valley of Newtondale and the heather-clad moors of Goathland to the harbour and ancient abbey at Whitby, a journey on the NYMR can offer a unique experience.

For the railway enthusiast, too, the NYMR is a special place. Engineered by none other than George Stephenson and promoted by Yorkshire's king of 'Railway Mania', George Hudson, before his spectacular fall from grace, few heritage railways can offer such diversity of scenery and motive power. There is some impressive infrastructure, including Stephenson's original tunnel at Grosmont, which once echoed to the sounds of horse-drawn trains, and through which today's visitors can walk to the extensive locomotive sheds. There are beautifully restored stations, each depicting a different era in the line's rich history at Grosmont, Goathland, Levisham and Pickering, with its magnificent newly reinstated overall station roof.

A favourite outing is to catch the train from Grosmont to Goathland, then follow the signposted Rail Trail. This trail takes you down the route of the original Stephenson rope-worked incline to Beck Hole, where the unique and characterful Birch Hall Inn is well worth a visit. The walk then continues alongside the Murk Esk to the cottages of Esk Valley, and eventually past the engine sheds and over the hill through which the railway tunnels into Grosmont.

The rope-worked line lasted almost thirty years, being replaced by the 'Deviation' route in 1865, climbing at a steady 1 in 49, and crossing spectacular waterfalls near Beck Hole on a series of bridges, one of which was replaced at huge cost in 2010.

When we used to go camping in Goathland in the early 1980s, the area was relatively quiet, but the appearance of ITV's *Heartbeat* series, set in 1960s Goathland (as Aidensfield) and featuring the railway in many of its episodes, drew and continues to draw huge numbers of visitors to the moors. Goathland station has since been the setting for Hogsmeade station in the Harry Potter films, the destination of the Hogwarts Express from Platform 9¾ at King's Cross.

When the great George Stephenson surveyed the original route in the 1830s, he faced some serious engineering challenges, and today's NYMR footplate crews face the challenge of coaxing their engines up 3 miles of 1-in-49 gradient from Grosmont to Goathland, which is hard work for the most powerful of locomotives.

It was in the late 1970s that our dads first introduced us to the delights of the NYMR and, as visits became more frequent, we fell in love with the place. When the Deltic Preservation Society's locomotives arrived in 1982, we volunteered at the railway and signed up as trainee firemen. As well as volunteering on the Deltics, which were our main interest, we also learned how to clean, light up and fire steam locomotives, and got our hands dirty on tasks such as needle-gunning the inside of a Black Five's tender water tank. We also got to appear on a BBC documentary about the railway.

Volunteering on the railway was amazing fun, and always felt like a privilege. Mark still does it now at Goathland station, where he is project managing the construction of a new station shop sympathetic to the original architecture of 1865.

Volunteer accommodation ranged from damp, cold compartments in corridor coaches parked in sidings to the Station House by the level crossing at Grosmont, which is now the station shop. Conditions were primitive but we didn't care.

Pub crawls to Egton Bridge, Goathland and Beck Hole were a feature of the evenings, which involved long walks and invariably a lock-in. We had to sign on at the shed about 4.00 a.m. to commence cleaning and lighting up of whichever locomotive we were rostered on. In those days it was not unusual to see ex-industrial tank locos in service, which were not very exciting – but at

KSHIRE

NAY

Cessford

First published 2016

Amberley Publishing
The Hill, Stroud
Gloucestershire, GL5 4EP

www.amberley-books.com

Copyright © Colin Alexander and Mark Cessford,
2016

The right of Colin Alexander and Mark Cessford
to be identified as the Author of this work has
been asserted in accordance with the Copyrights,
Designs and Patents Act 1988.

ISBN 978 1 4456 6184 1 (print)
ISBN 978 1 4456 6185 8 (ebook)

British Library Cataloguing in Publication Data.
A catalogue record for this book is available from
the British Library.

Typesetting by Amberley Publishing.
Printed in the UK.

least they were easy to clean. Occasionally, though, we would get something like the K1 or *Leander* with much more surface area to work on, and a much bigger firebox to look after. Colin remembers being rostered to fire the K1 as she worked tender-first from Pickering, and it was hard work up the 1 in 49 to Goathland summit, while Mark had the task of second-manning *Leander*.

We felt like grimy gods on the footplate, as admiring children and adults looked up at our black faces. Best of all were the bacon and eggs fried in the firebox on the special shovel, the tea in the white billy-cans and the bottles of Theakston's Old Peculier as a reward at the end of hard shift.

We had set aside the last day of May and the first day of June 2016 to take some photographs specifically for the book, aiming to cover as many missing locations as possible. To say the weather on those days was unseasonal is an understatement, so perhaps you will forgive the misty and grey nature of some of the photographs included, but rest assured that the sun does come out in Yorkshire sometimes!

Thanks must go to the NYMR's Peter Fisher, John Bruce, Paul Middleton and Chris Cubitt for their cooperation.

All photographs are by Colin Alexander and Mark Cessford, except where otherwise credited.

Ex-London North Eastern Railway K4 2-6-0 No. 61994 *The Great Marquess* runs around her train at Pickering, 26 August 2015. She is the sole survivor of a class of six powerful Moguls designed by Sir Nigel Gresley specifically for the steeply graded West Highland line. As such, she is eminently suitable for the NYMR's gradients.

When Gresley's much-maligned successor Edward Thompson retired in 1946 he was replaced by Arthur Peppercorn, whose first new design was the A2 mixed-traffic 4-6-2. We are fortunate that one example, No. 60532 *Blue Peter*, is preserved. The Pacific is seen here at the southern extremity of the NYMR at Pickering in 2002.

In August 1981, the North Eastern Locomotive Preservation Group's ex-North Eastern Railway Raven Class T2 0-8-0 No. 2238 runs around her train at Pickering. Mainly due to the great Dai Woodham of Barry, the GWR, SR and LMSR are well represented in preservation compared to the LNER, so we are very grateful to the likes of the NELPG for saving such unique machines for posterity.

In contrast, this scene taken thirty-four years later sees United States Army Transportation Corps Baldwin 2-8-0 No. 6046 under Pickering's new roof on 20 September 2013. The replica roof replaces the original, which was demolished in 1952. No. 6046 was one of over 2,000 such locomotives built for use in Europe during the Second World War. She saw post-war service in Hungary and is now based at the Churnet Valley Railway.

In May 2013 Pickering station's magnificent new roof amplifies the sound of A4 4-6-2 No. 60007 *Sir Nigel Gresley*, named after her legendary designer, as she arrives from Grosmont. In our opinion the early BR express blue livery really suits the Gresley Pacifics, especially when matched with carmine and cream ('blood and custard') coaching stock.

Pickering, on 5 October 2013, sees the impressive outline of Britain's newest mainline steam locomotive. The A1 Steam Locomotive Trust built No. 60163 *Tornado* at Darlington, and she made her debut in steam in 2008. The ornate screen at the end of the station roof frames the picture perfectly.

Ex-Southern Railway Class S15 4-6-0 No. 825 is seen entering Pickering station on 18 June 2013. No. 825 has the boiler from sister No. 841, whose frames are considered beyond repair. It is worth spending some time at Pickering station, with its fascinating and educational visitor centre and demonstration signal box – both recent additions.

The Great Marquess is seen again at Pickering in August 2015 beneath one of the NER's distinctive footbridges. This one came from Monkwearmouth station, north of Sunderland, when the station was remodelled and incorporated into St Peter's Metro station. The period lighting and luggage add to the authenticity of the scene.

Beyer-Peacock Hymek diesel-hydraulic D7029, owned by the Diesel Traction Group, spent some years on the NYMR, but is now at the Severn Valley Railway. She is one of four preserved. Here in 1981 she is arriving at Pickering, in the days before the platform was extended and when the carriage sheds were yet to be built.

The NYMR Diesel Galas are always worth a visit, and the September 2011 event featured unusual visitors from the Southern Region in the shape of Electro-Diesel No. 73136 and Class 33 D6515. The home fleet is represented here by No. 31128, double-heading with No. 37264 as they arrive at Pickering from the north.

Pickering in May 2013 sees No. 60007 *Sir Nigel Gresley* contrasting with Thompson B1 61264, masquerading as No. 61002 *Impala*. No. 61264 had a charmed life, going into departmental service after withdrawal and then finding her way to Woodham's scrapyard at Barry. Over 200 steam locomotives eventually escaped from the scrapyard, but No. 61264 was the only LNER-designed locomotive to do so.

Gresley's successor Edward Thompson made some controversial decisions in his time, but one of his successes was the B1 Class 4-6-0, 410 of which were built starting from 1942. One of only two survivors, No. 61264 is an engine of many guises and, in July 2014, she carried the identity of No. 61034 *Chiru*. The remains of Pickering Castle are visible above the locomotive.

The Deltic Preservation Society was fortunate to be able to use the NYMR as a first home for No. 55009 *Alycidon* and No. 55019 *Royal Highland Fusilier* from 1982 until about 1990. Here we see No. 55009 arriving at Pickering from Grosmont in about 1984, with matching blue-and-grey stock and a load of 'bashers' hanging out of the windows. The carriage shed is under construction in the background. (Ian Beattie)

Arguably the NYMR's 'flagship', No. 60007 *Sir Nigel Gresley* shows off her sleek lines when seen here broadside from the carriage depot at Pickering in 1998. The small plaque on her streamlined cladding commemorates her post-war steam speed record of 112 mph, achieved in 1959. The NER water column completes the scene.

Near the trout farm between Pickering and New Bridge is an overflow car park, which provides the vantage point for this unusual shot of BR Standard 4MT 4-6-0 No. 75029 as she passes in 2013. This lightweight class was designed for mixed traffic on routes where weight restrictions prevented heavier locos such as Black Fives from operating. Six are preserved.

If the B1s were the LNER's utility locomotive, then Stanier's Black Five 4-6-0s were definitely their equivalent on the London Midland & Scottish Railway. Passing over New Bridge level crossing, just outside Pickering on 17 October 2014 was No. 44806, built at Derby Works in 1944 and purchased by the NYMR in 2013, having previously been based at Steamtown, Carnforth and the Llangollen Railway.

Framed by the speed restriction sign at Levisham, No. 60007 *Sir Nigel Gresley* waits for the NER slotted lower-quadrant signal to drop at the head of the NYMR's luxury dining train in October 2013. This is a superb experience, with excellent service, food and drink provided in opulent surroundings. The first two vehicles are the ex-Great Western Railway saloon and the 1928 *Queen of Scots* Pullman car.

With a rake of Gresley teak coaches behind her, Peppercorn A1 4-6-2 No. 60163 *Tornado* is captured at Levisham in October 2013. Peppercorn's A1s were a development of his A2 class, as in *Blue Peter*, seen earlier. They were longer and had larger driving wheels but, despite their modern features and success, all were scrapped.

Sister to No. 44806, No. 45428 was built at Armstrong-Whitworth in Newcastle-upon-Tyne in 1937 and was named in preservation *Eric Treacy* in honour of the famous clergyman and railway photographer. No. 45428 is pictured in July 2014 waiting to leave Levisham, which is the first stop from Pickering, a distance of 6 miles.

Former Lambton, Hetton and Joicey Colliery Railway 0-6-2T, built by Robert Stephenson & Hawthorn in 1909, No. 5 is seen arriving at Levisham in 1981. This extensive private railway system was absorbed by the National Coal Board and had its own major locomotive workshops at Philadephia, near Washington, County Durham.

The handsome profile of Western diesel-hydraulic D1062 *Western Courier* is shown to good effect as she arrives at Levisham during the September 2013 diesel gala. BR's design panel and Sir Misha Black collaborated on the styling of this iconic class, a big improvement aesthetically on some of its predecessors. Seven survive in preservation including D1015 *Western Champion*, which is passed for mainline operation.

Levisham again, 1981 with Beyer-Peacock Hymek D7029, about to 'cross' with the Gloucester Railway Carriage & Wagon diesel multiple unit that was used for a long time by the NYMR for its 'Scenic Land Cruise'. The DMU has not fared well since, with two cars having being scrapped; the other pair still exists at the Midland Railway Centre.

A few passengers look expectantly to see what will be on the front of their Pickering train as Hymek D7029 waits at Levisham in 1981. This shot was taken from the level crossing, which is the only means of getting from one platform to the other here. Levisham station is a mile or so down a very steep hill from the pleasant village of the same name.

Making a distinct change from the LNER steam, here we have ex-Great Western Railway 0-6-2T No. 6619 at Levisham in 2001, heading a short train of vintage stock. This class was mostly associated with coal trains in the valleys of South Wales. No. 6619 is now undergoing overhaul at the Kent & East Sussex Railway after many years in North Yorkshire.

BR Standard 4MT 4-6-0 No. 75029 arrives at Levisham, bound for Pickering on 22 July 2014. Tender-first running does not normally lend itself to photography but the BR2 tender, designed to improve rearward view for the crew, somehow seems more photogenic. No. 75029 has carried the name *The Green Knight* since her early preservation days, when she was owned by David Shepherd.

Not looking quite as 'at home' on the teak stock as the LNER steam locomotives is English Electric Type 1, Class 20 No. 20189, passing over the level crossing at the north end of Levisham station in August 2015. Built as D8189 in 1967, she was one of a batch of 100 Class 20s ordered ten years after the original batch of 128 to replace the Clayton Class 17s, which proved to be disastrously unreliable.

The same location in October 2013 sees Barry-survivor Thompson B1 No. 61264 again, as No. 61002 *Impala*. The first forty-one of the class were all given names of antelopes. No matter what disguise she is wearing, it is always a pleasure to see No. 61264 in service. She has come a long way from serving as a stationary carriage-heating boiler in the 1960s and rusting away in Barry scrapyard.

Soon after her long-awaited return to steam following a lengthy and expensive rebuild, legendary LNER Gresley A3 Pacific, No. 60103 *Flying Scotsman* is seen passing Levisham's distant signal on a run from Grosmont to Pickering on 17 March 2016. The ninety-three-year-old treasure finally passed into the National Collection in 2004 after more than forty years in the hands of a succession of private owners, beginning with the great Alan Pegler in 1963.

On a fine day, this is a spectacular view looking down into Newtondale Gorge from Skelton Tower, a Victorian folly built as a shooting lodge by an eccentric Levisham vicar. Appearing through the unseasonal mist and drizzle of 1 June 2016 is BR Standard 4MT 2-6-0 No. 76079, heading for Pickering.

The more adventurous passenger can step off the train at remote Newtondale Halt where signs warn walkers of the presence of adders! This seems appropriate as the railway itself snakes through the glaciated gorge of Newtondale. English Electric Type 3 No. 37264 arrives at the halt on 31 May 2016, the driver stopping the train for us when we stuck out our hand, just like a bus stop.

Newtondale is a request stop. Anyone wishing to get off there must inform the train guard. In this May 2013 shot of apple-green Thompson B1 No. 61306 *Mayflower*, the guard is using the green flag to signal to the locomotive crew that there are no Newtondale passengers on board.

Just north of Newtondale Halt, another good lineside vantage point is Needle Point, at least on a clear day. Ex-NER Class T2 0-8-0 No. 63395 of 1918 is passing on a wet, cold and windy 31 May 2016. The passengers would be grateful for the steam-heating.

The powerful T2s were classified Q6 by the LNER, and No. 63395 is seen again on a much finer day in August 2015 passing a typical North Eastern Railway milepost as she threads her way through the heather and ferns of Newtondale Gorge.

This September 2014 shot of the National Railway Museum's Deltic No. 55002 *The King's Own Yorkshire Light Infantry* gives an idea of the dramatic scenery of Newtondale Gorge, through which the railway passes between Levisham and Goathland. Over the years riding the trains through Newtondale, we have glimpsed deer, heron and birds of prey here.

The curvature of the line is seen to good effect as A1 No. 60163 *Tornado* powers across Fen Bog with the beautifully restored Gresley teak set in October 2013. Here, George Stephenson and his men employed the ingenious solution of floating the permanent way on a bed of sheep fleeces to conquer the boggy terrain.

One of the stalwarts of NYMR operations is BR Sulzer Type 2 D7628, named *Sybilla*. She was built in 1965, and is one of twenty preserved from the original class of 327. Moments before this shot was taken through the mist at Fen Bog on 31 May 2016, we saw a pair of deer only about 100 metres away from us.

Also on 31 May 2016 at Fen Bog, by the time late-running Q6 No. 63395 appeared, I was soaked through and quite fed up! The LNER's 'Q' prefix denoted the 0-8-0 wheel arrangement: 'A', as in A4, was 4-6-2, B 4-6-0, and so on. This replaced some of the haphazard classification systems used by pre-grouping companies.

Her hard work over, Black Five No. 44806 is seen again on 17 October 2014 as she descends from Goathland Summit past Moorgates towards Goathland station. Above the train, and running in front of the cottages, can be traced the route of the original Stephenson line as it deviates from the present route. The surrounding scenery is magnificent at any time of year, but I think the autumnal colours show the National Park at its best.

This bridge, which is just hidden from view in the previous photograph, is a relic of the original 1836 Stephenson line, which crossed the road in Goathland village just to the west of the Goathland Hotel. North of the village, it descended steeply to Beck Hole using a rope-worked incline then followed a relatively level course beside the Murk Esk to Grosmont.

Thompson B1 4-6-0 No. 61264 passes Moorgates on 31 July 2014. Compare the parallel boiler and round-topped firebox of the LNER design here, with the taper boiler and square-shouldered Belpaire firebox on Stanier's design on the next page. Stanier borrowed from Great Western practice, having served at Swindon before moving to the LMSR.

Stanier 'Black Five' 4-6-0 No. 45428 *Eric Treacy* passes Abbots House, just south of Goathland, in July 2014. The railway here bisects a friendly campsite, and a little further north is another, where we and our mates enjoyed regular camping trips in our teenage summers. The lavatory on the station platform at Goathland was the closest facility!

Life doesn't get much better than this. Colin's two sons are sitting beside their tent as Gresley A4 No. 60007 *Sir Nigel Gresley* heads for Pickering in July 2014, with the LNER Gresley teak rake. She is about to pass one of the railway's NER slotted-post lower-quadrant signals. This is the approximate point where the wooded valleys and farmland to the north give way to moorland and glaciated gorge to the south.

Colin's love affair with No. 4472/60103 *Flying Scotsman* began in about 1969 when, at the age of five, he was taken by his dad to see her, complete with double tenders, at Newcastle Central station. Forty-seven years later, on St Patrick's Day 2016, she is seen setting out from Goathland towards Pickering through a suitably green landscape, with some of North Yorkshire's ubiquitous sheep in the foreground completing the scene.

A little closer to Goathland, in the summer of 1984, Peppercorn K1 2-6-0 No. 62005 heads for Pickering with a rake of blue-and-grey coaches, including some of the experimental XP64 stock of the 1960s. This shot was achieved by poking the camera through the fence right next to our favoured campsite of the time, later to be used as Claude Greengrass's farm in *Heartbeat* on television.

The weekend of 8 March 2015 saw the NYMR mark the occasion of the fiftieth anniversary of the line's closure by British Railways. Immaculate Stanier 'Black Five' No. 45428 *Eric Treacy* was used to haul the dining Pullman, seen here having got 'the board' to depart Goathland for Pickering.

The handsome lines of Gresley's masterpiece, the NRM's A3 Class 4-6-2 No. 60103 *Flying Scotsman* are seen to good effect at Goathland on 13 March 2016, in one of her first public appearances following her multi-million-pound restoration. Opinion has always been divided on the aesthetic merits of the 'German' smoke deflectors, but personally we don't mind them with BR green livery.

The distinctive and ornate North Eastern Railway signals that guard the southern approach to Goathland have allowed No. 37264 to pass as she arrives from Pickering on 31 July 2014. The signalling department is one of many in which volunteers can become involved.

A busy scene at Goathland on 8 March 2015, during the gala to mark the fiftieth anniversary of BR closure. 'Black Five' No. 45428 *Eric Treacy* makes a very smoky entry into the station from Grosmont alongside the Metropolitan-Cammell diesel multiple unit. It is highly likely that this DMU passed under the footbridge regularly when the structure was in situ at Howdon-on-Tyne.

Same locomotive, similar view, taken more than thirty years earlier. No. 45428 is seen departing Goathland with a lot less smoke in 1983. In those days, passengers had to use the barrow crossing at the north end of the station but, as the railway and Goathland in particular grew in popularity, the footbridge became a necessity.

B1 No. 61264, still carrying its No. 61034 identity, waits at Goathland on 31 July 2014. Great imagination has been used in catering for visitors here, as they can drink tea in Hull & Barnsley Railway open wagons inside the 1865 NER goods shed, and there are plans to create a picnic area on the pleasant lawns beside the water tower on the right.

Goathland's 'new' footbridge is seen straddling a train hauled by new-build Peppercorn A1 No. 60163 *Tornado* in October 2013. Having succeeded in achieving the construction of a complete mainline steam locomotive, the same group is now building a Gresley P2 2-8-2, which will if anything be an even more incredible sight.

BR 4MT No. 76079 is seen on a demonstration freight train at Goathland on 7 May 2016 during a Scottish-themed weekend. She is carrying the identity of Scottish Region sister No. 76001. These temporary re-numberings are usually achieved by the application of self-adhesive vinyl numerals.

The tank engine equivalent of No. 76079 was the 4MT 2-6-4T, of which fifteen are on heritage railways; there are currently three on the NYMR. No. 80072 had arrived quite recently when pictured from the footbridge at Goathland on 28 May 2016. There are examples of purpose-built wagons for the conveyance of gunpowder and molasses in the background.

BR 4MT 4-6-0 No. 75029 arrives at Goathland from Pickering on 13 April 2014, British Railways built a total of 999 locomotives of 'Standard' types from twelve designs between 1951–60, but scandalously all were withdrawn by 1968 in the indecent haste to dieselise at all costs. BR paid the price though, as many of the early diesels were temperamental to say the least.

Goathland on 8 March 2015 is the setting for Gresley K4 No. 61994 *The Great Marquess* and Peppercorn K1 No. 62005 double-heading the 'Whitby Moors Rail Tour'. Remarkably, almost exactly fifty years earlier, the same two locomotives had headed a train with the same name over the line. The 1965 tour originated in Manchester and was hauled as far as Wakefield by Jubilee No. 45698 *Mars*.

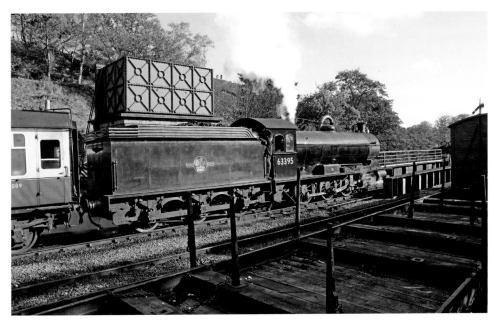

Ex-NER T2 0-8-0 No. 63395 is seen in the sunshine from the new viewing platform at Goathland in October 2014. Throughout her forty-nine-year working life, she and her sisters must have hauled millions of tons of coal and other freight, but she was fitted with vacuum brakes and steam-heating for passenger work by her new owners, the North Eastern Locomotive Preservation Group, before moving to the NYMR in 1970.

We make no apology for including another view of Gresley A3 4-6-2 No. 60103 *Flying Scotsman* at Goathland on 12 March 2016. Her fireman has just collected the single-line token to Levisham from the signalman. The roadside verges for miles around were totally clogged with parked cars, which belonged to photographers eager to capture the reborn legend.

The only two surviving Thompson B1s of the 410 built, No. 61264 (running as No. 61002) and No. 61306 *Mayflower* pass at Goathland in May 2013. The name 'Mayflower' was originally carried by long-scrapped classmate No. 61379. They were brought together for the gala weekend celebrating the preserved railway's fortieth anniversary.

Heritage railways give the visitor the opportunity to observe traditional operating practice in a way that is no longer possible on today's electronic mainline network. The fireman of 'Black Five' No. 44806 is seen here passing the single-line token for the Grosmont–Goathland section to the signalman in April 2014. The train cannot proceed without the token for the section to Levisham, which will be on board the northbound train, soon to arrive.

Here we can see the Goathland signalman handing the token to the driver of BR Sulzer Type 2, Class 24 D5061 as she arrives from Pickering on 20 September 2013, passing No. 45428 *Eric Treacy*. D5061 is one of only four survivors of this class of 151 diesel-electrics, and two of them are at the NYMR. Sister D5032 has been undergoing restoration at Grosmont for many years now.

It is hot and thirsty work on the footplate of a steam locomotive, and the crew of 'Black Five' No. 45428 take advantage of the station stop at Goathland to grab a well-earned cup of tea. The date is 20 September 2013. Some drivers and firemen use the traditional enamel 'billy can', which sits on a shelf immediately above the firebox door.

Two of English Electric's finest at Goathland during the September 2013 diesel gala. Class 37 No. 37264 heads a southbound service and waits for Type 5 'Deltic' D9009 *Alycidon* to clear the single-line section. Although to the casual passer-by they appear similar, internally they could not be more different. The Class 37, with its single, slow-speed 1750hp engine, actually weighs more than the Deltic with its twin Napier engines generating 3300 hp.

The volunteer crew of No. 63395 pose for the camera in this Goathland scene on 17 October 2014. The railway is always looking for enthusiastic volunteers in all sorts of roles, not all as glamorous as footplate crew. One of the most rewarding days Colin ever spent was working in a permanent-way gang at Levisham in the freezing winter of 1982, with hot stew provided to keep everyone going.

The Gresley duo of A4 No. 60007 *Sir Nigel Gresley* and K4 No. 61994 *The Great Marquess* pass at Goathland on 8 March 2015. Like most preserved lines, the NYMR is single track, with facilities for trains to pass at Levisham, Goathland and Grosmont.

Goathland on 18 September 2010 sees the arrival of D5061, which had an interesting history. She was withdrawn from BR stock as No. 24061 as early as 1975, and transferred to Derby's research department, being renumbered ADB968007. She later became No. 97201 *Experiment* and was used to haul a variety of test trains until final withdrawal in 1987.

The wide-angle lens accentuates the gentle curvature of the layout as No. 60007 *Sir Nigel Gresley* rolls into Goathland from Grosmont on 8 March 2015. In reality, the station provides only a brief respite for locomotives and crews as the gradient continues beyond the station to Goathland summit, a couple of miles further south.

Metropolitan-Cammell diesel multiple unit *Daisy* stands at Goathland on 8 March 2015, the occasion of the fiftieth anniversary of closure. DMUs such as this were used on the line in latter days, as they were on many rural routes in an attempt to economise. Sadly, this did not prevent the 'Beeching Axe' falling on many much-loved lines.

Riddles' BR Standard 4MT 2-6-0 No. 76079, nicknamed the 'Pocket Rocket', arrives at Goathland from Grosmont in April 2004. This versatile class was based on Ivatt's earlier Mogul for the LMSR, and examples of both types operated in the North-East in BR days. They were regular performers on the famous Stainmore route between Darlington and Penrith.

The unique eight-wheeled bogie tender of Southern Railway S15 4-6-0 No. 825 is clearly shown as she arrives at Goathland with a Pickering train on 18 June 2013. This is the view from the footbridge; in the sidings behind the platform stands one of the camping coaches, one of which is available as a holiday let while others provide accommodation for volunteers.

The architectural style typified by Goathland is seen at most stations along the Esk Valley line to Whitby, and was also used in parts of County Durham. No. 55002 *The King's Own Yorkshire Light Infantry* looks somewhat incongruous in this rural setting during a diesel gala on 13 September 2014.

Goathland is one of the best-known heritage railway locations in the UK today, having starred as Hogsmeade station in the Harry Potter films and Aidensfield in television's *Heartbeat*. Swindon Warship D821 *Greyhound* is captured there on 14 September 2013, next to the site of the new shop being built by volunteers.

Most British industrial railways relied on 0-4-0 and 0-6-0 tank engines but the Lambton, Hetton & Joicey system in County Durham ran a fleet of powerful 0-6-2 tanks. Thankfully, two of them are preserved at the NYMR and we can see Kitson-built No. 29 of 1904 storming up the last few yards of 1-in-49 gradient into Goathland station on 29 July 2014.

An unusual visitor in 2002 was one of Bulleid's Southern Railway 'air-smoothed' light Pacifics, No. 34081 *92 Squadron*. This class was the lighter version of the Merchant Navy Class, and were named after either locations in the West Country or on a Battle of Britain theme. The striking malachite-green and sunshine-yellow livery completes the eye-catching appearance.

Passengers observe as Southern S15 4-6-0 No. 825 strides up the last few yards of the incline into Goathland on 18 June 2013. The path at the top right leads over the hill to that favourite photographic location, Darnholm, seen on the front cover, and which we will see again shortly.

At the same spot we have the stirring sight of LNER Mogul double-header, K4 No. 61994 and K1 No. 62005 arriving at Goathland on 8 March 2015 with the 'Whitby Moors Rail Tour'. The term 'Mogul' refers to the 2-6-0, in the same way that 'Pacific' denotes a 4-6-2. These were internationally recognised terms.

Having assisted No. 61994 to Pickering, No. 62005 provided the 'tail' of the 'top-and-tail' formation on the return trip on 8 March 2015. The train is descending towards Grosmont, which requires skilful brake work on the part of the locomotive crew.

During the Scottish Region-themed event, Birmingham Railway Carriage & Wagon Type 2, Class 26 No. 26038 arrives at Goathland on 7 May 2016. Based on one of the more successful 'pilot scheme' diesel designs, this class spent most of its life in Scotland, although the first examples began their careers in North London.

On descending from Goathland towards Grosmont, the line passes the idyllic location of Darnholm, where Peppercorn K1 2-6-0 No. 62005 is seen in 1983. There is a bench on which to enjoy a flask of tea while waiting for trains, and there is a ford where you can cool your feet on a hot day.

A closer view at Darnholm, where No. 44806 is seen carrying a headboard reading 'The Preston Rambler' on 2 July 2014. It is quite unusual to see locomotives running light engine like this. A total of 842 Black Fives were built by the LMSR, BR and private contractors. No. 44806 was built at Derby in 1944 and is one of nineteen to survive in preservation.

In September 2013, Thompson B1 4-6-0 No. 61264 (as No. 61002 *Impala*) makes a fine sight as she storms up the gradient past Darnholm with the 'Yorkshire Coast Express'. Darnholm is one of the best photography vantage points lineside, and is a short walk from Goathland station.

On the same date, again at Darnholm, all is not what it seems. BR Standard 4MT 4-6-0 No. 75029 is in fact the 'tail' of a 'top-and-tail' working with No. 45428 *Eric Treacy* at the head of the train, just out of sight around the curve. No. 75029's safety valve is lifting as she coasts effortlessly down the 1-in-49 gradient.

Accessible from a footpath off the Beck Hole road, there are a number of viewpoints beside the Murk Esk river. BR 4MT 2-6-0 No. 76079 coasts down the bank, having just crossed bridge 30 on a dull and drizzly 1 June 2016. This bridge had recently been replaced at great expense.

On the same damp 1 June 2016, No. 37264 climbs towards bridge 30, having just passed the waterfalls named Nelly Ayre Foss and Thomason Foss. There is a path from Beck Hole village that follows the river upstream to the waterfalls, but it is only for the adventurous and those without fear of heights!

The lack of turning facilities means that, in one direction, steam locomotives have to travel tender-first or bunker-first. None of them look more wrong than an A4. The distinctive porthole illuminating the narrow passage of her corridor tender can be seen, as No. 60007 *Sir Nigel Gresley* passes Beck Hole in July 2014 as she drifts downhill towards Grosmont.

Another aspect of volunteer work is lineside clearance, as evidenced in this March 2016 view of No. 45428 *Eric Treacy* passing Beck Hole. Clearing lineside trees is not carried out for the benefit of photographers. One reason is to reduce the age-old autumnal problem of leaves on the line, which can cause a train to wheel-slip to a standstill on the 1-in-49 gradient here.

The change in colour with the change in season is evident as No. 37264 passes Beck Hole on 1 June 2016. When the bright 'large logo' livery first appeared on some BR diesels and electrics in the 1980s, it made a welcome change from the monotonous plain blue that had dominated.

Later that same day, 1 June 2016, No. 37264 is seen further down the incline at Green End. Colin is visible in this shot, standing in field taking the next photograph …

… while Mark can just about be spotted on the old occupation bridge at Green End, taking the previous photograph! By now we'd had two days of standing in damp fields in continuous drizzle, but were revived at regular intervals by cups of tea at station cafés and, best of all, coffee and beer cake in the wonderful Birch Hall Inn at Beck Hole.

Rosebay willowherb grows in profusion along Britain's railway lines, and the NYMR is no exception. It is July 2014 and B1 No. 61264 is rolling downhill past Green End towards Esk Valley and Grosmont. The twisting route of the line allows frequent opportunities for shots like this, although leaning out of the train window is not, of course, recommended.

In contrast to the last three views of trains coasting down the grade, BR 4MT 2-6-0 No. 76079 is using every ounce of her strength as she climbs past Green End on 1 June 2016. The steam-heating is obviously being used in the coaching stock. This is not normally necessary in June!

The sound of a steam locomotive grappling with the 1-in-49 incline out of Grosmont is something to behold, and No. 60007 *Sir Nigel Gresley* is working hard here on the heavy dining Pullman train past Esk Valley in October 2013. Her 6-foot, 8-inch-diameter driving wheels were designed for the East Coast Main Line and not for slogging up steep gradients in the Yorkshire hills, but she takes it in her stride.

The multi-coloured terraced cottages of Esk Valley, passed on the Rail Trail walk to Goathland, form the background to this view of Q6 0-8-0 No. 63395 climbing towards the viaduct on 1 June 2016.

BR Standard 4MT 2-6-4T No. 80135 makes a fine sight as she leaves Grosmont behind and heads for Esk Valley in 1983. For any shot like this, the photographer must be in possession of a lineside permit and be wearing a high-visibility vest.

At the same spot, also in 1983, is the Deltic Preservation Society's No. 55019 *Royal Highland Fusilier* leaves behind an impressive cloud of exhaust as she accelerates up the gradient. No. 55019 is another remarkable preservation story, in that she has operated in all but one of her thirty-four years since being rescued by the DPS in 1982. (Ian Beattie)

Two days of damp had, by this point, caused Colin's camera to completely fog up internally. So, improvising as usual, this not-to-be-missed shot of the volcanic Q6 No. 63395 passing the end of Grosmont headshunt at beginning of the climb to Goathland summit on 1 June 2016 was taken using his mobile phone!

As your train slows for the approach to Grosmont, a long headshunt is alongside the running line on the eastern side. It is used for the storage of locomotives awaiting their turn for restoration, such as BR Standard 9F 2-10-0 No. 92134 and 4MT 4-6-0 No. 75014, seen in 1982. No. 92134 still has not steamed, and is now being worked on at Crewe. No. 75014 is more fortunate, having since appeared on the main line.

An NYMR regular at the time, 0-6-0T No. 31 *Meteor*, built by Robert Stephenson & Hawthorn for the NCB in Northumberland, passes Grosmont headshunt in 1983. Colin took the photo while working on the roof of one of the DPS Deltics. This would not be permitted today, next to a running line. Mark, meanwhile, was on the footplate of *Meteor*, which is now at the East Somerset Railway.

War Department Austerity 2-10-0 No. 3672 *Dame Vera Lynn* is seen on the headshunt at Grosmont in July 2014. She was built for the British Army by North British in 1944 and was shipped to Egypt, before being sold for service in Greece. She is currently the subject of a fundraising campaign to restore her to working order.

The early 1980s saw some unusual diesel types arrive on the railway, none more so than Clayton Class 17 Bo-Bo D8568, having been rescued by the Diesel Traction Group; she is seen here with D821 about 1992. D8568 outlived her 116 scrapped classmates, which were all withdrawn from BR by 1972, in industrial use at Ribble Cement, Clitheroe. She is now based at the Chinnor & Princes Risborough Railway.

Grosmont headshunt again in 1983, with the Peppercorn K1 carrying the attractive but incorrect LNER green livery and the number 2005. Like her sisters, she was delivered after nationalisation in black as BR No. 62005. Beyond her are Deltic No. 55009 *Alycidon* and Hymek D7029.

0-6-0T *Jennifer* was often used as a 'banker', providing rear-end assistance up to Goathland; however, by 1981, she was out of use in Grosmont headshunt, sandwiched between 9F No. 92134 and a Southern Railway van. Built by Hudswell Clarke in 1942 for Samuel Fox, a Sheffield steel company, *Jennifer* is now at the Epping Ongar Railway in Essex.

The intricate pointwork leading from the headshunt into the locomotive yard at Grosmont forms the foreground of this shot of No. 37264 on 31 May 2016. We were kindly given permission to take photographs in and around the shed area.

A powerful study of USATC S160 Class 2-8-0 No. 6046 passing the same spot, also on 31 May 2016. She is getting into her stride as she leans into the curve and builds up speed to tackle the gradient. One of the railway's two 45-ton steam cranes can be seen on the right.

In complete contrast, Drewry diesel-mechanical shunter, BR Class 04 D2207, stands outside the Deviation Shed in 1984, with the same crane in the background. The shed is named after Deviation Junction, so called because this is where the 1865 route deviated from the original 1836 horse-drawn line.

Inside the North Eastern Locomotive Preservation Group's Deviation Shed, the National Railway Museum's Q 7 No. 63460 is seen undergoing restoration *circa* 2000. Built by the North Eastern Railway to a design by Sir Vincent Raven, this class of fifteen three-cylinder 0-8-0s were best known for working the 700-ton iron-ore trains up the steep gradients from Tyne Dock to Consett.

If you walk the well-signposted Rail Trail from Goathland along the route of George Stephenson's original 1836 line through some delightful scenery, you are eventually rewarded with good views of the sheds at Grosmont. BR Sulzer Type 2 D5032 is seen here about 1981.

The streamlined profile of Gresley A4 4-6-2 No. 60007 *Sir Nigel Gresley* is seen from above as she stands outside the Deviation Shed in July 2014. BR Class 08 diesel-electric shunter No. 08850, of which over 1,000 similar were built, is alongside.

Behind the Deviation Shed on 31 May 2016 is BRC&W Class 26 No. 26038 alongside Deltic No. 55022 *Royal Scots Grey* appearing as sister locomotive No. 55007 *Pinza*. This was more than a self-adhesive vinyl change of identity, as it also involved painting the cab window surrounds white, changing the nameplates and plating over the headcode panels at each end. Some might call it sacrilege.

Also at Grosmont, pioneer English Electric Type 3, Class 37 D6700 is part of the National Collection, and was a guest at the 2014 diesel gala. This versatile and long-lived class has been seen on all kinds of workings, including china-clay trains in Cornwall, heavy coal and steel trains in South Wales and north-east England, passenger trains in the Scotland Highlands and even, experimentally, in pairs on high-speed West of England services.

June 2013 sees Southern Railway S15 4-6-0 No. 825 under the coaling stage at Grosmont shed. Over the years, the locomotive shed area has evolved piecemeal. At the beginning of the preservation era, the NYMR locomotive fleet was based at Goathland, but a lack of space there prevented further development. The public viewing areas of Grosmont shed are well worth a visit.

In its early days, the NYMR, like many preserved lines at the time, relied on industrial tank engines to maintain its services. Lambton Tanks Nos 5 and 29 arrived from Philadelphia in County Durham in 1970, and are seen together at Grosmont about 1978. Nowadays they have fewer duties, as more powerful locomotives are needed for the heavier trains. (John Alexander)

During the Fortieth Anniversary Steam Gala in May 2013, another Black Five No. 44871 negotiates the sharp curve as she passes Grosmont shed. No. 44871 has gone down in history as one of the locomotives used on 11 August 1968's 'Fifteen Guinea Special', bringing down the curtain BR steam. The others were sisters Nos 44781 and 45110, along with 'Britannia' Pacific No. 70013 *Oliver Cromwell*. Of these, only No. 44781 did not make it into preservation.

Some idea of the sheer scale of the work done at Grosmont shed can be gained from this pair of shots of Southern Railway Maunsell-designed Schools Class V No. 30926 *Repton*. In this first view she is seen awaiting a boiler overhaul in 2015. This is another locomotive with an interesting history: after withdrawal from BR, she spent time in the USA and Canada before repatriation in the late 1980s.

And here we can see the upturned boiler of No. 30926 being worked on inside the boiler shop at Grosmont on 31 May 2016. It is possible to make a guided tour of the shed at certain times, and it is fascinating to see what goes on behind the scenes.

In the running shed area of the complex, the smokebox door of Q6 No. 63395 is open as her blastpipe receives attention at Grosmont on 31 July 2014. One of the dirtiest jobs of the locomotive crew is emptying the smokebox of ash at the end of the working day.

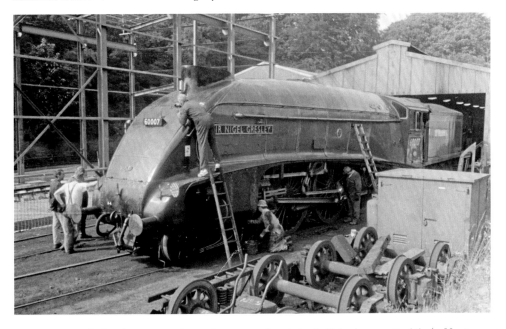

Grosmont's new boiler shop seen on the previous page is here being built in about 1996, while A4 No. 60007 *Sir Nigel Gresley* is worked on in the open air. Today, of course, all of the volunteers working on the locomotive would be wearing high-visibility clothing.

J72 Class 0-6-0T No. 69023, resident at the line in 1983, was one of a batch of twenty-eight built by BR in the 1950s to a Worsdell North Eastern Railway design dating back to the 1890s. The Victorian cottages beside Grosmont shed were sadly later demolished to make way for expanded locomotive facilities.

Tucked in behind No. 69023 on the same day was a high-profile visitor to the railway in the shape of ex-LMSR Stanier Jubilee Class 4-6-0 No. 5690 *Leander*. She is one of four survivors of a class of 191 built for express passenger services all over the Midland network. Mark was lucky enough to be trainee fireman on her for a day.

GNR 0-6-0ST No. 1247, LNER Class J52, was notable in being the first BR steam locomotive to be bought privately by an individual, although she is now in the National Collection. She spent some years on the NYMR, and is seen here in about 1978 at Grosmont shed in the company of K1 No. 2005. (John Alexander)

Hymek D7029 and 4MT 2-6-4T No. 80135 stand outside Grosmont shed in 1981 under a smoky atmosphere courtesy of Q6 No. 63395, then carrying her NER number, 2238. This scene is transformed now, with the demolition of the cottages and the building of the boiler shop.

The high-visibility clothing reflects the camera flash as BR Standard 4MT 2-6-4T No. 80072 stands over the well-lit inspection pit inside Grosmont shed on 31 May 2016. 'Black Five' No. 44806 is alongside. Both of these classes were very successful and versatile designs, and were seen almost everywhere on the BR network.

The bodywork of BR Type 2, Class 24 D5032 is undergoing some major work during a lengthy overhaul, as seen here inside Grosmont shed on 31 May 2016. The Sulzer 1160-hp engines employed both in classes 24 and 26 were uprated to 1250 hp for use in the later derivations, classes 25 and 27.

Just beyond D5032, as we look out from inside the shed on 31 May 2016, the tender end of BR 4MT 2-6-0 No. 76079 is viewed as she is prepared for her duties. Beside her is an English Electric diesel-electric 0-6-0 shunter, numbered 12139. She is to the same design as BR Class 11, but she was built for ICI at Wilton on Teesside in 1948.

NYMR favourite, BR 4MT 2-6-4T No. 80135, is in the middle of a complete overhaul deep inside Grosmont shed on 31 May 2016. Her left-hand cylinder can clearly be seen, as can the space between her large water tanks where her boiler should be.

An unusual view from the shed area through the tunnel to Grosmont station in October 2014 has captured ex-NER T2 LNER Q6 0-8-0 No. 63395 threading her way over the crossover to take the running line as she departs for Pickering. Grosmont was actually known as Tunnel in the days when the village boasted its own ironworks, of which very little now remains.

No. 63395 again, in NER livery, as No. 2238 stands alongside an unlikely stablemate in the shape of Swindon-built diesel hydraulic D9520 at Grosmont in 1981. These Paxman-engined 650-hp 0-6-0 Type 1s were built for short-trip freight workings on the Western Region. After a ridiculously short career on BR due to those workings disappearing, most found further employment in industry and even abroad.

From this angle on 31 May 2016, newly arrived BR Standard 4MT 2-6-4T No. 80136 looks complete, but closer inspection reveals that not only does she lack a cab roof but, more importantly, she is awaiting the return of her boiler. She should be in traffic by the time this book is published.

The driver of Hymek D7029 begins to apply the 1700 hp of her Maybach engine to her torque-convertor as she accelerates past Grosmont shed in 1981. Class 24 D5032 is just visible to the right. The NYMR was certainly a haven for fans of British Railways' early diesel locomotives at this time in the early 1980s, and the Deltics were yet to arrive!

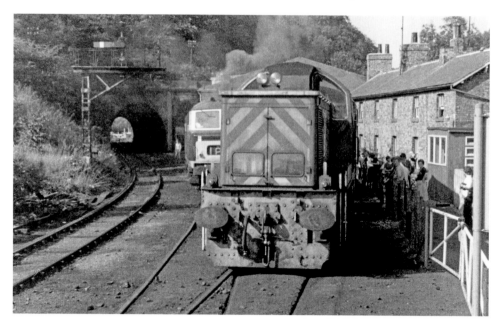

D9520 is seen again moving off the shed in front of Hymek D7029 in 1981. D9520 was built at Swindon in 1964 and, after less than three-and-a-half years in Western Region service, she was sold to British Steel at Corby where she worked until 1981. She is now at the Nene Valley Railway, not far from her industrial home.

As you can see, in 1981, the footpath in front of the old railway cottages meant the public could get up close to the locomotives on shed at Grosmont, such as BR Standard 4MT 2-6-4T No. 80135. These cottages were very much part of the facilities, featuring a temperamental coal-fired shower for the locomotive crews.

Another visitor at Grosmont, this time in May 2013 inside the shed, is ex-LMSR Stanier Black Five 4-6-0 No. 45407. Only four out of 800-plus Black Fives carried names in service, which is surprising for such a successful and popular class. No. 45407 is carrying the name *The Lancashire Fusilier*, derived from the name of Royal Scot No. 46119 *Lancashire Fusilier*.

Outside Grosmont shed on 5 October 2013, Lambton Tank No. 29 gleams in the autumn sunshine. Compared to number 5, No. 29 had a low, curved cab roof for clearance through the narrow, low-roofed tunnel to the coal staithes on the River Wear. Parts of Standard Mogul No. 76079 are visible on the right.

Three hours later, and No. 29 now has a fire lit and A4 4-6-2 No. 60007 *Sir Nigel Gresley* for company at Grosmont on 5 October 2013. The pair are old acquaintances from when the A4 was based at NCB Philadelphia in the early 1970s.

A second Swindon Type 1, Class 14 D9529, which, like D9520, also came from British Steel, is seen leaving Grosmont station in 1983, viewed from above the tunnel with the bridge over the line to Whitby in the distance. Steep hills are a feature of the villages in the area, as participants in the recent Tour de Yorkshire cycle race discovered.

Having emerged from the north portal of Grosmont tunnel, Gresley K4 2-6-0 No. 61994 *The Great Marquess* is now crossing the bridge over the Murk Esk and is about to rumble over the level crossing into the station. The date is 26 August 2015 and the photograph is taken from the specially constructed viewing platform.

It is 6 May 2013 at Grosmont and the occasion is the fortieth anniversary of the NYMR. BR Standard 4MT 4-6-0 No. 75029 is making a dramatic departure for Pickering. In a moment she will plunge into the tunnel before facing the 3-mile slog at 1 in 49 up to Goathland. The aforementioned viewing platform can be seen on the right, with the Grosmont floral display on the left.

The September 2013 diesel gala saw the welcome return of Warship D821 *Greyhound* to the line; she is seen here in a running-around manoeuvre at Grosmont. The Warships were victims of BR's standardisation policy and were prematurely withdrawn by the early 1970s. They were unique in being a German design, the DB V200, being shoehorned into the restrictive British loading gauge.

War Department Austerity 2-10-0, numbered 90775, was resident on the line for a while; she is seen here departing Grosmont for Pickering in about 1996. BR had a fleet of over 700 slightly smaller 2-8-0s, along with twenty-five ten-coupled locomotives like this. No. 90775, however, had served in the Middle East before passing to Hellenic State Railways in Greece. She is now at the North Norfolk Railway.

In July 2014, BR Standard 4MT 4-6-0 No. 75029 is seen between duties, bathed in beautiful sunshine under a blue sky at Grosmont station. Locomotives of this class in BR service were mostly seen in the south and west of England and Wales, although some lasted until the end of steam in 1968 in the Skipton and Carnforth areas.

In April 2004, Peppercorn K1 No. 62005 is captured on the level crossing at Grosmont. The Station Tavern is behind the locomotive. Many a night was spent in here when volunteering on the line. If we were short of cash, we would set off on pub crawls to Egton Bridge, Goathland and Beck Hole, involving a 6- or 7-mile walk up and down hills in pitch darkness.

Colin's favourite steam-locomotive type of all, Gresley V2 2-6-2 No. 60800 *Green Arrow*, is seen at Grosmont during a visit to the line in about 2001. As well as being extremely aesthetically pleasing, the V2 is a highly capable design, the class of 184 famously being dubbed 'the engines that won the war'. It would be wonderful to see her back in working order again.

The Deltic Preservation Society's No. 55019 *Royal Highland Fusilier* is slowing for the platform at Grosmont with a train from Pickering in 1983. The two Deltics were popular on the line, but difficulty of access for DPS volunteers in the south led to the eventual establishment of a purpose-built depot for them at Barrow Hill in Derbyshire.

A long-time NYMR resident locomotive was this one-off variant of the ubiquitous Black Five, No. 44767, pictured at Grosmont in about 2000. She is unique in being fitted with Stephenson valve gear instead of the Walschaerts or Caprotti gear, and was named after the great Tyneside engineer, George Stephenson, at the Stockton & Darlington Railway's 150th anniversary celebrations at Shildon in 1975.

B1 No. 61264 proudly shows off her early BR 'cycling lion' emblem as she stands beneath an impressive array of semaphore signals at Grosmont in July 2014. The village of Grosmont has clearly benefited from the increased numbers of visitors attracted by the railway, as there are now many more shops, cafés and so on than existed in the 1970s and '80s.

An East Coast giant from an earlier era, LNER A4 4-6-2 No. 60007 *Sir Nigel Gresley* stands at Grosmont in 2014. Colin has many childhood memories of this locomotive, thanks again to his dad, who took him to see her passing Haydon Bridge and Low Fell on railtours, to NCB Philadelphia where she was based, and to Thornaby open day in 1972 where she was the star attraction.

The National Collection's pioneer Brush Type 2, D5500, poses alongside AC Cars railbus W79978 at Grosmont about 1978. The four-wheeled railbus had been at the NYMR for about ten years, but was by this time far too small. It is now at the Colne Valley Railway in Essex. D5500 now wears its later blue livery and her later number 31018, and is on display in the National Railway Museum in York. (John Alexander)

Former resident of the NYMR, and enjoying a welcome return for the 2013 Diesel Gala, the Diesel Traction Group's BR Warship Class diesel-hydraulic D821 *Greyhound* is seen running around her train at Grosmont. Almost as powerful as and 55 tons lighter than the Peak shown below, D821 was the first privately preserved BR mainline diesel locomotive and she now resides at the Severn Valley Railway.

The September 2010 gala featured BR Sulzer Type 4 Class 45 No. 45041 *Royal Tank Regiment*. This class of 127 locomotives was used extensively on the Midland main line out of St Pancras as well as on the north-east to south-west route from Newcastle to Birmingham and beyond.

With their graceful streamlining, it is no wonder Gresley's A4s have such legendary status. As built, Gresley's A4s were even more glamorous with their deep valances over the motion; these were removed during the Second World War for ease of maintenance. No. 4464 *Bittern* has had hers restored and looks stunning at Grosmont during a gala appearance in May 2014. (Helen Cessford)

Here is No. 60007 *Sir Nigel Gresley* again, at Grosmont in 2013. Two A4s were shipped to North America in the 1960s but, remarkably, they were temporarily repatriated in 2012, and externally restored to take part in a reunion of all six survivors at Locomotion, Shildon, for the seventy-fifth anniversary of the famous 126-mph world speed record established and still held by No. 4468 *Mallard*.

By the early 1980s, the days of small ex-industrial tank engines running NYMR services were almost over, as longer trains were needed to cope with growing passenger traffic. This 1983 shot at Grosmont shows Austerity No. 3180 *Antwerp* awaiting departure for Pickering. We both cleaned, lit and fired this locomotive on several occasions. Built by Hunslet in 1944 for the War Department, she was then sold to the National Coal Board.

A momentous occasion at Grosmont on 21 August 1982, as a preserved Deltic is about to haul a passenger train for the first time. The Deltic Preservation Society's No. 55009 *Alycidon* and No. 55019 *Royal Highland Fusilier* stand side-by-side the day after their arrival from Doncaster. No. 55019 did the first 36-mile round trip to Pickering, followed by No. 55009.

An unusual view of Grosmont station from the footbridge that crosses the Esk Valley line from Middlesbrough to Whitby. K4 No. 61994 awaits her next duty at the platform in August 2015, while the gas lamp, level-crossing gates and red telephone box help to set the scene. The entrance to the pedestrian tunnel leading to the engine shed is visible in the background.

In 1981, Warship D821 stands at Platform 3 at Grosmont, ready for departure. These were good times for fans of diesel-hydraulics at the Moors, with the Warship, Hymek and the pair of Class 14s. On one memorable occasion, we travelled the length of the line and back on a train 'top-and-tailed' by the Warship and Hymek – almost 4000 hp of Maybach power.

A powerful low-angle shot taken in May 2013 of Black Five No. 44871 at Grosmont's Platform 2, which was lengthened a few years ago to accommodate longer trains. Passengers who wish to get off the train at Goathland, Newtondale or Levisham have to follow the polite instructions of NYMR staff and sit in certain parts of the train, as those stations have much shorter platforms.

Gresley's handsome West Highland Mogul No. 61994 *The Great Marquess* again, in a photograph taken on 26 August 2015. The rear of the coach carries a Network Rail tail-lamp, and forms a through service to Whitby. Only locomotives and coaches that are equipped and certified for mainline use are permitted to proceed beyond this point.

Another diesel-electric in use at Grosmont in 2013 was Brush Type 2 Class 31 No. 31128. Developed from the original 'pilot scheme' class of 20 (see D5500 earlier), a further 243 had been delivered before it was decided that their Mirrlees engines needed to be replaced by more reliable English Electric power units. Delivered in 1959, she lasted a whole fifty years in service, being withdrawn in 2009.

Black Five No. 45428 *Eric Treacy* is the subject in this wider-angle shot at Grosmont, taken in July 2014. It is becoming increasingly difficult to take photos here without people getting in the way, due to the railway's deserved popularity, but some would argue it is the people who complete the composition. I wonder what legendary photographer Eric Treacy himself would have said on the subject?

Seen without the smoke deflectors that are such a prominent feature of S15s, Southern No. 825 stands at Grosmont in April 2004, alongside the Pullman diner. The S15s were designed for heavy freight and, with her 5-foot, 7-inch driving wheels, No. 825 is ideal for the hilly NYMR. The name Grosmont, incidentally, comes from the former monastery here, once populated by French monks, of which there is now no trace.

J72 0-6-0T No. 69023 is waiting to depart for Pickering in this shot taken in 1983. Although most of her sisters were, in BR days, painted plain black, at least two wore North Eastern Railway green, as seen here, for station pilot duty at Newcastle and York. Black Five No. 45428 is being steam tested alongside in undercoat – something else that seems unlikely today!

This study of ex-NER T2 LNER Q6 No. 63395 on 17 October 2014 shows that she was built for heavy freight haulage, with small diameter wheels with no leading bogie or pony truck, which means all of her weight is available for adhesion. Notice also the short-coupled wheelbase to cope with tight curves; those small wheels are ideal for hauling heavy trains up the incline to Goathland.

A very unusual visitor to the 2014 Autumn Steam Gala is 0-6-0PT No. 1501. This is the only surviving example of a class of ten, designed by Hawksworth for the GWR and introduced in 1949, the last and most powerful in a long line of Great Western pannier tanks. After a short career handling empty stock in and out of Paddington, she was sold to the NCB and now resides at the Severn Valley Railway.

The NYMR diesel galas invariably feature types that would never have appeared on the line in BR days, and the 2011 event was no exception – although D6515 may well have got as far as York in the days when pairs of the class were employed on the Cliffe–Uddingston cement trains. BRCW Type 3 Class 33 D6515 is one of ninety-eight built specially for the Southern Region of BR.

Another Black Five photographed at Grosmont in April 2015, once again of No. 45407; however, a broader view is on offer this time, showing the signal gantry that controls access to the Esk Valley line to Whitby. The trees in the left distance are on the site of Grosmont's Victorian ironworks, which only lasted thirty years and had disappeared by the end of the nineteenth century.

A pleasing broadside shot of B1 No. 61306 at Grosmont in May 2013. Locomotives of the 4-6-0 wheel arrangement were the mixed-traffic workhorses on most British railways after Jones introduced the first on the Highland Railway in the 1890s. Only the GWR favoured this wheel arrangement for its top-link express locomotives, though, the other 'Big Three' preferring Pacifics.

The elegant profile of new-build A1 4-6-2 No. 60163 *Tornado* is seen to advantage in this October 2013 shot at Grosmont. It could have been so different, after Edward Thompson famously rebuilt Gresley's original 1922-built A1 No. 4470 *Great Northern* into an ungainly looking prototype. Thankfully Thompson retired before they were put into production and Peppercorn's handsome A1s were introduced instead.

Superpower at Grosmont in August 2011, with BR Standard 9F Class 2-10-0 awaiting departure. Colin has never known a steam locomotive climb to Goathland as effortlessly as this machine did. She is now at the Great Central Railway in Loughborough. The only 9F named in BR days was of course the last one, No. 92220 *Evening Star*, the *Cock O' The North* name coming from Gresley's legendary P2 2-8-2, now being recreated by the same team that built *Tornado*.

Under a clear blue sky at Grosmont in July 2014, Thompson B1 4-6-0 No. 61264 (as No. 61034 *Chiru*) builds up steam in readiness to do battle with the incline to Goathland. Grosmont station carries the attractive blue, cream and tangerine colours of BR's North Eastern Region.

Another fine study of A4 No. 60007 *Sir Nigel Gresley* at Grosmont in October 2013. We would like to dedicate this photograph to the memory of Marjorie Hamilton, who loved the A4s and the Deltics, and was a great friend to and supporter of the NYMR, the A4 Locomotive Society and Deltic Preservation Society.

In September 2014, the National Railway Museum's English Electric Deltic No. 55002 *The King's Own Yorkshire Light Infantry* is seen under the same gantry. The Napier Deltic engine is an incredible piece of British engineering with its eighteen cylinders and three crankshafts. Other applications for the power unit included naval minesweepers and even an American fire tender pump!

The high-running plate for ease of maintenance was a trademark of the BR Standard steam locomotives, as exemplified by 4MT 2-6-0 No. 76079 as she arrives at Grosmont from Whitby in March 2015, on the occasion of the fiftieth anniversary of the line's closure by BR. A few members of this class were allocated to the North Eastern Region and were used on the famous Stainmore line between Darlington and Penrith.

English Electric Type 1 Class 20 No. 20189 is seen under the signal gantry at the north end of Grosmont station in August 2015, with the Whitby line disappearing around the bend and the GWR observation saloon in the siding. With their lack of train heating, the Class 20s were always a rarity on passenger services when we were young but, each summer, they were guaranteed to appear on holiday trains to Skegness.

Comparison between this August 1981 photograph of Hymek diesel-hydraulic D7029 and the view below shows how drastically the track layout has changed at Grosmont Junction. The white buffer-stop is approximately where No. 61994 is standing in the 2015 photo, and the BR line to Whitby is on a different alignment altogether.

Thirty-four years later and we have a much busier scene at the junction end of Grosmont, taken in August 2015. K4 No. 61994 *The Great Marquess* stands at Platform 2 with an arrival from Pickering, as Black Five No. 45428 *Eric Treacy* is about to swing across the double-slip into Platform 3 with a Whitby–Pickering service. The line to Battersby and Middlesbrough is straight ahead of No. 45428. Class 25 D7628 stands by, ready to take No. 61994's train forward to Whitby.

The stylish profile of Beyer-Peacock 'Hymek' Type 3 D7029 is glimpsed at Grosmont Junction in August 1981. Like the Warships and Westerns, the Hymeks were another versatile and successful Western Region class that was withdrawn long before they were life-expired, due to standardisation.

Beyond Grosmont Junction, the NYMR shares Network Rail metals as far as Whitby. English Electric Class 55 Deltic No. 55022 (as No. 55007 *Pinza*) passes Sleights in charge of a Whitby–Pickering service on 31 May 2016. The modern road bridge spans both the railway and the River Esk here.

A moment earlier, No. 55007 is seen passing through the Northern Rail station at Sleights, which only has one platform in use now. The station building is now in residential use and is undergoing some major maintenance.

Trains between Grosmont and Whitby run alongside the River Esk and, as Whitby is approached, the impressive Larpool viaduct can be seen. This structure once carried Middlesbrough–Scarborough trains along the coastal route, which was a victim of the 'Beeching Axe' in the 1960s. A steep spur connected the surviving terminus of Whitby Town with the higher level Whitby Westcliff station on the Scarborough line.

The Deltic Preservation Society's mainline registered D9009 *Alycidon* at Whitby in September 2013, just over thirty-one years after making her preservation debut at Grosmont. At this time, NYMR services had to share the single platform with Northern Rail trains from Middlesbrough, and had to be top-and-tailed, or to reverse to the passing loop at the south end of the station for the locomotive to run around.

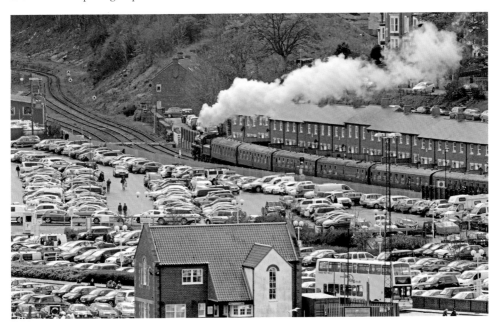

Today the NYMR has its own dedicated platform and run-around facility at Whitby Town, replacing that so short-sightedly removed by BR. Seen from Whitby Abbey, 4MT No. 76079 has left from the new NYMR platform at Whitby in April 2016 with a train for Pickering. Can any other heritage railway offer such a journey, from an ancient seaport with its abbey to a market town with its castle, past waterfalls and heather-clad moors where deer roam?